The PhD Survival Guide

Lessons from Life and Lab

by Allan M. Grant

Copyright © 2018 by Allan M. Grant. All rights reserved.

ISBN: 978-1-9164629-1-5

No part of this book may be used or reproduced in any manner whatsoever without written permission except in the case of brief quotations for the purposes of critical review.

Published by Rising Tide Press

Rising Tide Press Limited,

71 – 75 Shelton Street,

Covent Garden,

London,

WC2H 9JQ

www.RisingTidePress.co.uk

Requests to publish work from this book should be sent to: enquiries@RisingTidePress.co.uk

Cover created by Sophie Lees Design

sophie.lees-design@outlook.com

Scientist image designed by Freepik

Table of Contents

How to Use this Book.. 5

1. Introduction: Understanding the Landscape............ 8
2. Application, Induction and Preparation...................13
   Funding Challenges: My Experience 15
   Fail to Prepare and Prepare to Fail!..........................18
3. Getting Started: The Train Has Left the Station! ... 20
   Initial Considerations... 20
   Your Supervisory Team: Dynamics, Responsibilities and Expectations... 22
   Tools of the Trade 26
   The Confirmation of Registration 28
4. Ethics, Recruitment and Data Collection 32
   Research Ethics Application and Approval............. 32
   Participant Recruitment 35
   Data Collection: The Bread and Butter................... 37
5. Challenges and Progression: Embracing Reality.... 40
   Participant Retention..41
   Infrastructure.. 42
   Progression Meetings.. 47
6. Data Analysis and Interpretation 49
7. Writing for Publication and Thesis Submission 52
   The Working Environment 52
   Academic Journals: The Unit of Currency.............. 54
   Conference Proceedings.. 58

- The Role of Feedback 59
- Capitalise on Your Work! 60
- 8. Preparing for the Viva 63
- 9. Strategies for Optimal Health and Wellbeing 66
  - Annual Leave: Make Use of Your Entitlement 66
  - Develop a Routine 67
  - Health, Exercise and Nutrition 70
  - Read Widely! 73
  - Managing Relationships 75
- 10. Risk Parity Principles 78
  - Build an Emergency Fund 78
  - If Possible, Publish! 80
  - Be Accountable and Document Everything 81
  - Learn to Say 'No'! 82
  - Extensions and 'Writing Up' 83
  - Consider Employment Avenues Early On 84
- 11. Enhancing Employability 86
- 12. Closing Remarks 91
- Further Reading 93
- Useful Links 95
- About the Publisher 96

How to Use this Book

The process of completing a laboratory-based PhD, with human participants in particular, is one of the most difficult and challenging pursuits that the prospective student will ever undertake. There will be moments of incredible reward and achievement, contrasted with others of supreme challenge and self-doubt.

My intent with this guide is to impart strategies to help you along the path, drawing on my experiences both in the lab and in my personal life. This book should be used as a 'primer' of sorts for those of you about to set out on the journey. Once you're under way, it can be used as a reference guide to accompany you at key stages.

Sadly, I've known several individuals that were forced to drop out of their PhD studies for numerous reasons; some self-inflicted and others whereby circumstances simply conspired against them. A group of colleagues overran their deadlines by a considerable margin due to these assorted factors, and some of these examples are discussed here. Hopefully, this book will help minimise the likelihood of such adverse events occurring, smooth out the volatility, and make the journey more gratifying and fruitful as a result.

I've structured the text to address the typical PhD framework, beginning with the application and induction phase, and ending with the viva voce examination. In each section, typical issues and concerns are addressed, with strategies provided from a number of logistical and psychological standpoints. Contentious issues and challenges are discussed at length to provide insights and learning opportunities. I advise you to make notes, formulate your own ideas, critically appraise them, and ultimately apply this knowledge throughout your PhD.

This guide refers to PhD degrees in the biological and health sciences, given my background in these areas, however most of the content will apply to PhD students in a far broader sense. This is also true for regional irregularities; although the United Kingdom is referred to quite frequently, most of the advice will be universally applicable around the world.

This book refers to several websites and I have provided links to these sources in the text. At the time of writing these were active pages, however I cannot be held responsible in the event that these are broken or inaccessible following publication.

I hope you find the book helpful and I wish you the very best of luck in your studies!

1. Introduction: Understanding the Landscape

For those aspiring to a career in academia, perhaps as a researcher or lecturer, the attainment of a PhD degree is rapidly becoming an essential prerequisite. This is certainly the case in the United Kingdom, from personal experience. A cursory glimpse at job specifications and person descriptions on www.jobs.ac.uk[1] will verify this beyond all doubt. Therefore, if this career path is indeed your goal the necessity of a PhD is unavoidable, and merely a sign of the times. Nevertheless, before engaging in any endeavour it is crucial to investigate the field or discipline of interest and assess the nature of the task at hand. Perhaps more importantly, you need to be absolutely sure of your desire to undertake what can be

---

[1] See useful links.

an unforgiving and brutal challenge, in light of the benefits it might confer.

In completing a PhD, the student will acquire the skills and knowledge to perform independent research - essentially building the foundations of an academic career. Unfortunately, the present job market is so densely populated with graduates that an undergraduate degree is no longer satisfactory to merely walk into employment, at least not in an abstract sense. This is not an isolated issue in academia - since the New Labour policies of the late 1990s, there has been huge growth in the number of undergraduates in general, leading to an erosion in the value of these qualifications. In 2000/01 the total number of undergraduate and postgraduate degrees obtained was ~480,000, whereas in 2016/17 this was ~757,000, according to the Higher Education Statistics Agency[2]. The mechanics of supply and demand are not difficult to comprehend here - the sheer abundance of undergraduates and a shortage of roles in which to employ them are the defining hallmarks of this phenomenon. Therefore, the graft that high-achieving students put in to obtain their first-class honours degrees, in useful fields no less, may not be

---

[2] https://www.hesa.ac.uk/data-and-analysis/students/outcomes.

recognised with meaningful employment and progression.

Regrettably, there are signs that postgraduate degrees are also being 'debased' in this manner. Students, myself included, proceed directly into postgraduate courses following their first degree, and who can blame them? They're merely advancing their knowledge, making themselves more employable and striving to distinguish themselves from the rest of the crowd. In my own case, whilst studying full-time I found it tremendously difficult to acquire a decent part-time job and avoid living off my meagre savings. I eventually relied on loans from my parents to get to the finish line. This experience will resonate with many postgraduates I'm sure. Irrespective of the time, effort and resources expended, it is exceedingly rare for those with postgraduate degrees to gain employment as a lecturer in higher education, if that is indeed their goal. Those that occupy such positions without a PhD seem to be declining year on year, signifying that they are a dying breed. I can count on one hand the number of academics I've known in senior positions without a PhD, and these have dwindled in line with prevailing trends. It won't be long before teaching-focused staff without a PhD are a thing of the past. Awareness and acceptance of this reality will allow you to prepare accordingly.

The attainment of a PhD is rather different from the former qualifications in that the student is supposed to make a novel contribution to the evidence base or 'the literature', with greater autonomy and independence of scholarship. Hence, the student is exposed to a range of skills that position them well for the academic career in question. Of course, this doesn't mean that a job at the end is guaranteed, it simply means that the student will have *the best chance of being competitive*. I'll discuss these elements in more detail later on, including how to enhance your employability whilst engaged with your PhD project, but in this day and age nothing is guaranteed. All you can do is manipulate the variables under your power!

The second major reason to pursue a PhD would be one's fundamental passion for their subject area. A genuine love for the topic will help you make a novel and original contribution to knowledge, whilst gaining valuable skills and experience along the way. In fact, I would propose that a PhD can't be effectively completed without a love for, or interest in, the topic area due to the sheer amount of work and sacrifice that's involved.

Lastly, most lab-based PhD courses place a great deal more responsibility on the student, often requiring them to teach undergraduates at a bare minimum. This can be developmental for your public speaking abilities and further enhances your CV. Students also receive training and invaluable exposure to advanced techniques and methods. If these elements are intriguing and you have a genuine passion for your field then PhD study could be the ideal way to go.

2. Application, Induction and Preparation

Now that you have established that the pursuit of a PhD is a noble and desirable one, the first challenge will be to win a studentship or stipend. This is likely to be the most desirable option - based on the circumstances of most candidates - and is the one I adopted for my own degree. In the United Kingdom, bursaries or stipends are provided for three or four years, depending on whether the position involves teaching commitments as part of a graduate teaching assistantship (GTA). These opportunities are few and far between, with many requiring the student to work on an established project in a supervisor's area of expertise. These projects are usually set up under a recognised infrastructure, and the PhD tends to follow on from a previous student's work. In the final analysis, you are essentially furthering a 'dynasty' of research, which may or may not be an attractive proposition, depending on your attitude and world view.

The requirements for studentships are usually listed - for example on FindAPhD or www.jobs.ac.uk[3] - alongside the project overview, background and supervisor details. Contingent on the discipline of study, you may be required to possess laboratory bench skills and have a strong undergraduate degree. As alluded to in the previous chapter, it is highly likely that a postgraduate degree will also be necessary. If you possess any publications in academic journals, these will help substantially in your application. You will also be required to conduct some preliminary scholarship for the application in the form of a research proposal. This is no small task and will require a decent amount of work on your part to set out a viable rationale, methodology and context for the project. Your mileage may vary, depending on the research discipline, but be ready to invest some substantial time and resources.

Choosing an institution will largely be a decision based on geography, the nature of the supervisory team, the facilities on offer, the type of project and whether it is self-funded or not. As you'll see below, if a scholarship is

---

[3] See useful links for information on these sites.

absolutely necessary then the choice of location and PhD title will not really be under your power to influence. Ultimately, the project itself needs to be one you are happy with at this stage. You can deal with any subsequent considerations as you move through the process.

Funding Challenges: My Experience

After completing my undergraduate degree as a mature student (21 – 24 years old) and postgraduate degree immediately afterwards, I felt that my passion for research in the biological sciences would serve me well for PhD study. I had performed nicely in my academic studies up to that point in higher education, despite being average at school, and decided to strive for the next level. My only option was to pursue a funded studentship to bring this aspiration about, as I'd burned through my savings and capital to fund my postgraduate degree. I set about looking for suitable projects, contacting supervisors, and putting in applications to a range of universities around the United Kingdom.

In retrospect, my academic profile was mediocre in spite of my qualifications and I was unsuccessful in my applications for a couple of years. I had a number of interviews at various places, including some where I narrowly missed out on the position. Each of these applications involved a huge amount of scholarship and effort, not to mention travel demands and stress. Some of the applications were prepared six months ahead of the deadline, following conversations with the project supervisor and a tremendous amount of independent work, only to fail at the interview and presentation stage. In these situations, I found it best to take a step back, learn from the experience after critically reviewing everything, and then *move forward* as soon as possible. Get used to rejection, because it's extremely likely to happen! Once you've had time to reflect, approach the interview staff and/or project supervisor to get feedback, which will help you develop and improve.

I used these 'application years' to begin my teaching and research career, compiling a portfolio of experience as well as laboratory skills and academic journal publications. After multiple applications and interviews, I was nearly ready to call it quits and move back into the private sector. Ultimately I was successful after enhancing my profile, to excess in my opinion. I'd done a massive amount of work, much of it for free, but had at last managed to secure a position in an area of great personal interest. A number of circumstances aligned to bring this about: the nature of the project, my own skill set and experience, and the supervisory team all converging at the same time. I had also worked with the lead supervisor on a separate project that eventually led to a research publication, which was invaluable for the application.

I'm not suggesting that your journey will be as difficult or as lengthy as mine (in fact, I've seen other students walk into a bursary with just an undergraduate degree), I'm merely illustrating how competitive the environment can be. There are other factors at play, many beyond your intrinsic academic merit, such as political, monetary and organisational concerns. Your success may depend on ability, or perhaps serendipity, but regardless the best strategy is to accept the situation for what it is and reflect upon your failures to take things forward. Sometimes success is less about talent or hard work than merely your ability to tolerate what gets thrown at you, and this will be a recurring theme throughout life in general!

An alternative avenue for those without the capital or savings to fund their PhD on a full-time basis would be to study part-time and work at a separate job. This will present several difficulties, particularly during the data collection phase as you struggle to reconcile the demands of your job to support the 'hobby' degree you are trying to complete. I had several colleagues that worked in this manner, and whilst they were highly capable and conscientious students, they were faced with many unique and disparate challenges. The logistical and psychological stresses of working with human research participants, laboratory infrastructure, *and* separate employment can often be overwhelming and demands a highly resilient temperament. Students that opt for this approach will need an organised lifestyle and an especially diligent personality, allied with copious amounts of patience.

Once you've secured funding it's time to get on with the PhD in earnest!

Fail to Prepare and Prepare to Fail!

Most PhDs will commence in September, the start of the academic year in the United Kingdom. In the intervening period between formalising your studies and being given an office and so forth, it is invaluable to conduct background reading and solidify your early ideas and concepts. If you can sit down with your supervisory team for a meeting at all, this would be highly advised. Obviously, this will depend on your proximity to the institution. In so doing, you will be able to discuss the broad themes of the project and areas of focus ahead of the start date, so that you can hit the ground running when the clock starts ticking. A Skype meeting would work as a suitable alternative, and I strongly believe that this would be advantageous, as a bare minimum, before starting your studies proper.

3. Getting Started: The Train Has Left the Station!

In accepting a position as a bursary student or GTA, you have essentially left the station at Point Pleasant and are heading on a journey through the Mountains of Mayhem. The train needs to reach Submission Square in a timely manner, or the passengers and rail operator are likely to get annoyed. A number of incidents will happen along the way, some within your power, most of them not, and it's up to you as the driver to deal with these, by managing the elements under your control.

Initial Considerations

In the first week, you are likely to be familiarising yourself with the institution, its facilities, the local area, your supervisory team and other rudimentary aspects. Of particular importance will be your social group, as extracurricular activities will form a crucial backbone in times of stress. Therefore, spend a good deal of time building these foundations up. The first port of call will be to form strong connections within the institution, its staff, and your fellow research students. Explore your new town or city, ensure that your living conditions and accommodation are up to scratch, and befriend a select group of people from outside academia as well. You will need family and/or friends around that don't fundamentally understand what you're doing, to keep you grounded in some sort of everyday reality.

To reiterate, immersing yourself in the research community is paramount. These individuals, your fellow PhD students in particular, will be an indispensable asset throughout the process. Indeed, some will become lifelong friends. From my perspective, this is absolutely essential and one of the best things about doing a PhD. The camaraderie and feelings of mutual success, understanding and cooperation will persist long after your viva voce examination is complete.

Your Supervisory Team: Dynamics, Responsibilities and Expectations

You may be familiar with members of your supervisory team from communicating with them as part of the application process. The relationships and interactions between you, your director of studies (DoS) and supervisor(s) will shape the nature of the project, and can make or break the entire endeavour. They are the 'arbiters of fate' - much will depend on the individual personalities and temperaments within your group, and you will be meeting with them on a regular basis, at least in the first instance.

From the outset, there needs to be mutual understanding across all team members to bring about the best dynamic. As the student, you must feel able to raise issues and concerns with frank honesty and openness. If this is not the case, a great deal of resentment can build up, particularly if the DoS has substantial ownership over the project. In Russell Group universities for example, or studentships that have been brought about by grant funding, the DoS will retain an iron hand of control. You will essentially serve the role of pack mule, getting the work done and putting the hours in, without a meaningful input to the design and execution of the study. This is not inherently a bad thing, however you need to be aware of this before engaging with the process. After all, irrespective of what anybody says, *it's your PhD*. Fortunately, my own experience involved a balance of autonomy and authoritarianism. In the laboratory, I was able to crack on at my own discretion, whereas in terms of deadlines for papers and 'big picture' events, I had to work within agreed timeframes. This dynamic was compatible with my personality traits, and I advise that you adapt to your own team and tailor the dynamics to reconcile with your nature as well.

The crucial point I would like to stress is that you should *regard your team as peers, not staff*. Indeed, they are likely to possess more knowledge and experience than you in the beginning, but over the programme of study you will develop and grow quite dramatically. Many students form long-lasting friendships with their team, and this is the desirable outcome. However, events can occur that lead to a breakdown in communication between staff and student, so getting things right from the start is paramount. Discussing your concerns with a third party prior to involving the research office is always prudent, and there are likely to be procedures in place should you desire a change in supervision. At my institution, this was a rare occurrence, but you should be aware that options are available if you need to exercise them.

I witnessed a number of students run off the edge of the proverbial cliff, like Wile E. Coyote in the Roadrunner cartoons. They essentially kept the pedal to the metal and did not consider the implications for their PhD without their regular stipend coming in each month. This is easily done when caught up in the miasma of data collection, writing, teaching and so forth. Ideally, you will need an emergency fund while you secure part-time employment (I'll explain this later on in Chapter 10) to pay for the remainder of your studies. In these circumstances, the ideal team will act as a bedrock of support, as opposed to making you feel like you aren't worthy of your position.

It's perhaps worth mentioning that the interests of your team are not always your interests. As with many areas of life, this is not necessarily insidious; rather it is an objective reality that you need to embrace. Everyone has their own specific goals and motivations in their personal lives, business and almost any other discipline you can think of. Your team will want you to complete in the allotted timeframe to benefit from the research outputs and a tidy submission, all whilst squeezing as much productivity out of you[4] as the position allows. As the student, you should desire to earn a PhD before the funding deadline if possible. Therefore, conflicts may develop based on the interests of each party. For example, extra teaching commitments may be placed on you, or other more superfluous tasks that actively impede your progress, but benefit the team or research group. While this didn't happen to me, I know of several students that had to 'take a stand' to safeguard their PhD time. If necessary, you must do likewise for your own sanity and workload.

I would like to repeat that *it's your PhD*! If things go awry then it will be *your* head on the block, in the proverbial sense of course. In my view, the student assumes a significant proportion of the risk, and therefore should have some say in the direction and priorities of the project. You will need to ensure that the expectations of your team are realistic and achievable given the time, resources and infrastructure available. In return, you should expect creative, academic and pastoral support from them as dictated by their remit. They will have deployment hours allocated to facilitate this, so make the most of the opportunity. Their

---

[4] https://www.theguardian.com/commentisfree/2018/aug/15/should-do-phd-you-asked-autocomplete-questions.

expectations of you will be to engage fully (although this should be guaranteed, considering what you had to do to get the role!) and deliver on monthly objectives. The bottom line is for you to complete the PhD within the agreed timeframe, as stated in your contract. Notwithstanding the negative consequences that might transpire, in my own experience I found the mutual understanding and cooperation with my team to be incredibly rewarding, not to mention the intellectual discussions and updates in monthly meetings. If you can attain this dynamic for your own studies it will be highly beneficial, however you must always remain vigilant to the concerns and issues highlighted above.

Tools of the Trade

In the beginning, it's best to get your work environment organised to save aggravation later on when things are up and running. Make sure that you are provided with a good laptop or desktop PC, a telephone (or university Skype account), bookshelves, storage space and stationery items. There will be specific software programmes that are absolutely indispensable, for example:

- Microsoft Office suite (Word, Excel, and PowerPoint at the bare minimum)

- Microsoft Outlook/Google Mail (for planning, organisation and communication)

- Statistical analysis software (i.e., SPSS, R*, GraphPad Prism, and/or Matlab for example)

- Citation manager (EndNote, Mendeley)

Personally, I found a citation manager to be an absolute godsend. I used EndNote by Clarivate Analytics to compile references for my thesis, manuscripts, and general areas of interest. For my PhD thesis alone, I amassed more than 500 references and this would be very difficult to manage without such an application. Allied with Microsoft Word, references can be cited as you write and the software will build the bibliography for you. In addition, it is possible to export citations from databases (e.g., PubMed) and open them directly in your software library. This is tremendously powerful, especially for those students conducting systematic reviews and meta-analyses. EndNote has made me much more efficient and I strongly advise that you use it or a comparable alternative.

I will discuss the more organisational elements later on but the role of your email account and organiser cannot be understated, so be sure to maximise their utility. Certain websites can be of great fundamental value, such as ResearchGate and Academia.edu. These sites enable you to follow key scholars in the discipline of interest and stay up to date with recent papers and developments. Social media can also be very useful for this purpose, especially Twitter. Not only will these resources help you build a research presence, they are invaluable for collating your evidence base.

Finally, lab-based students will want to familiarise themselves with the facilities and equipment they are likely to use during data collection. This will make things easier later on when booking in participants and research trials. If you require specific skills or training, like phlebotomy (venepuncture) for instance, then strive to acquire these elements as soon as possible, using the appropriate channels.

The Confirmation of Registration

The Confirmation of Registration (COR) process ensures that your research design and objectives are deliverable within the specific timeframe and also serves to provide a degree of academic oversight. It involves writing a proposal to the research office outlining your rationale for the project, an overview of the proposed design and methodology as well as a timeline in which you aspire to deliver it. This is then processed by the research office and senior academics in the area, prior to a meeting with you and your supervisory team.

In the meeting, you will be grilled by academics with knowledge of the discipline alongside someone from a completely different field. This process can be gruelling for some and more pleasant for others, but nonetheless it is usually a highly developmental exercise. The university and its staff fundamentally want you to succeed and most, but not all, attendees of the meeting will be supportive and offer critical feedback. I know of two former colleagues that had regrettable COR meetings, during which one member of the panel tried to assert their academic prowess and was generally disparaging. Be aware that this is the exception and not the rule, and your own COR is likely to be a hugely beneficial event.

Several students (me included) enter PhD study with grandiose notions of bringing about a paradigm shift with their ground-breaking research. Unfortunately, this is rather unlikely to occur, except for a minute number of individuals. Therefore, many projects need to be trimmed, or streamlined, to allow the student to effectively deliver in the allotted time. It may feel like your wings are being clipped, but to be honest this process will help you in the long run. The chief goal should be the completion of a PhD-worthy thesis – anything more can be fleshed out and developed after your studies are complete. Personally, I found the interjections in my COR meeting to be reassuring and thought-provoking. They brought aspects to my attention that I had neglected to consider. Again, I know of other students that got metaphorically immolated and had to make major design changes to their research, so be prepared.

If you do your due diligence, given that you have three or four months to prepare, you should sail through the COR process. Once this document is signed off you are free to 'pass go and collect £200' as it were. The period between commencing your studies and passing the COR is a supremely valuable time. It is vital that you read around your topic area and fully immerse yourself in the literature, without the complications of data collection, manuscript writing and so on. The teaching commitments that you have (if applicable) will be highly developmental and you will be able to add these experiences to your 'employability portfolio'. Do your best to capitalise on this time and there will undoubtedly be segments of your COR document that you can use during the next phase.

4. Ethics, Recruitment and Data Collection

Research Ethics Application and Approval

Most, if not all, PhD students will be familiar with the ethical application and review systems given their studies at undergraduate and postgraduate level. Unless they were working on a staff project and didn't have to go through the processes in substantive detail, students will be cognisant of the procedures involved. Although specific to each university, in brief the student is required to submit a detailed synthesis of the research study in question. The number of studies that one conducts will be highly individual, so it's difficult for me to describe your precise experience here, but nevertheless each study will need to be ethically approved before data collection can commence.

The fundamental purpose of ethical review is to ensure oversight with regards to the research design and protocols that the investigator wants to conduct. For studies using human participants, the ethical review process will correspond with the standards of the Declaration of Helsinki[5]. This paperwork is usually very thorough and you will need to provide all relevant documentation as part of the submission.

There are three tiers of stratification:

- First tier projects tend to be systematic reviews and secondary data analyses, thus requiring only the approval of your DoS.

- Second tier studies require the approval of a Local Research Ethics Co-ordinator (LREC). These may involve human participants for example.

- Third tier studies might typically involve procedures such as blood and/or tissue sampling, and therefore require ethical approval at the faculty level. This may entail a meeting

---

[5] https://jamanetwork.com/journals/jama/fullarticle/1760318.

with the appropriate staff, however for the most part the entire process can be conducted using the university's online system.

Some UK-based students working with clinical populations will need to obtain ethical approval from the National Health Service (NHS) Research Ethics Committee. This process is substantially more thorough, at least in my experience, than anything conducted at the university level. My submission numbered ~70 pages in length and took several months to complete, from conception to approval. Contingent on the type of procedures you will be conducting, for example those that use ionising radiation (i.e. CT or DXA scans), the electronic signatures of qualified medical physics and clinical radiation experts will be needed, and these can take some time to obtain.

Once submitted, the review and approval process can be lengthy, culminating in a meeting with several medical experts and members of the lay public, where you will be grilled on a number of issues. Again, as with the university ethics procedures and COR, this event can be highly developmental and encourages you to communicate your research whilst considering both the practical and 'big picture' applications. What's more, the successful submission of an NHS ethics application will provide the student with valuable skills and experience that they can carry forward to post-doctoral positions and/or a research career.

Participant Recruitment

Once the study is ethically approved, the recruitment of participants and data collection phase can begin. You will already possess the information sheet from your ethics application alongside other relevant paperwork, such as promotional flyers and/or leaflets for instance. Therefore, you should have all the necessary elements to begin as soon as approval is granted.

In my studies I found several strategies that were highly valuable for recruitment and these are as follows:

- Leaflets can be useful provided they are well designed, eye-catching and communicate the key messages effectively. If you know someone with experience of graphical design or a similar field, they can help produce a quality leaflet. In all honesty though, most of my research participants were recruited using other means.

- Emails to the target populations of interest, for example organisations or social groups, can be a good entry point. Indeed, this was how I conducted most of my recruitment.

- If applicable, try to recruit participants from your social group and pay them back in kind. Obviously, these individuals will need to meet your inclusion criteria.

- Present your project at meetings and speak to interested parties face-to-face.

- Make use of social media to spread the promotional materials and garner support. This will depend of course on the reach of your profile – the university will often help with this as well.

- Contact the university public relations department and they will be happy to promote your project within the wider community and lay press.

- Give the participants you recruit every opportunity to promote the project within their social circles. If they have a positive experience they are highly likely to do this. Building rapport is key here!

Those students conducting research in clinical settings will have an easier time of recruiting, given the 'captive audience' of potential participants with the specific health condition or trait under study. For example, the student may be embedded in a hospital cardiology department and therefore have access to patients in this discipline. Some universities are partnered with teaching hospitals, and such collaborations offer useful opportunities in this regard, so do your best to capitalise on these.

Data Collection: The Bread and Butter

The simplest word to describe success during the data collection phase is *momentum*. That is to say, your turnover of participants is generally balanced with your ability to recruit them, and retention is maximised. Also, you will have all of the other elements in equilibrium, such as reading and teaching, so that one does not interfere with the other. This is extremely difficult and requires a great deal of organisation and luck. In addition, it is a great psychological challenge to shift between the data collection mindset and that of an academic scholar or teacher, within a very short timeframe, often a matter of hours. A good workaround for this is to have a break of an hour or two between these phases, and schedule this in your calendar or organiser.

In the early stages of this phase, it is recommended that you pilot your experimental protocol to iron out any deficiencies. In this way, you can optimise the process and make things considerably easier for subsequent trials. If you have support from other PhD students or postgraduates, these individuals will need to be briefed in the procedures and design as well. Once the protocol is locked in, the rest will take care of itself. It's a great feeling when a study is motoring along nicely, like clockwork, to the extent that it feels like you are flying on autopilot. It's extremely important to identify the potential areas that might cause the gears to grind, so that you can anticipate them and minimise their impact.

The following chapter addresses some of the main challenges that you will face during this phase, as it can take many months to complete. Indeed, you are likely to spend the bulk of your PhD in the data collection phase, depending on how many studies you are conducting and their level of complexity.

Not all institutions will facilitate this, but I advise it wholeheartedly – if you can collaborate in any meaningful way with other PhD students you will be able to share research outputs and learn new skills and techniques that you may otherwise not have access to. In addition, other PhD students can be tremendously helpful during the data collection phase to help you get the project completed on time, and in my experience this type of collaboration is mutually beneficial to all parties.

5. Challenges and Progression: Embracing Reality

A number of issues and obstacles will present themselves during your PhD, most of which will be beyond the realms of your control. The manner in which you deal with these concerns can make or break the PhD process. I will provide some case study examples from my own experiences and those of former colleagues below. As mentioned earlier, completing a PhD is *less about academic talent as it is hard work and your resilience to stress*. In getting to this point, you have already evidenced your conscientiousness and intelligence, so these prerequisites should take care of themselves. This chapter focuses on specific issues that might arise and proposes some strategies to lessen their impact.

Participant Retention

For any researcher involved in studies on living, breathing humans there are some harsh realities that you need to appreciate. Participants take part in projects of their own volition and, within the ethical framework discussed earlier, have every right to withdraw on their terms. This is irrespective of how much time and/or resources you have invested in them thus far.

In the short-term, flaky participants can be tremendously annoying if you've set up the lab and arranged support staff, leaving you to pack everything away and rebook for another day, provided the individual hasn't dropped out completely. Depending on your study design, if a participant withdraws 8 weeks into a 12 week intervention study, substantial resources and time will have been wasted. This is one of the most frustrating things about research of this nature, and there is ultimately nothing you can do about it. Therefore, it is imperative to form strong and empathetic relationships with your participants, so that they feel invested in the project and are aware of its wider impact and applications. I can't stress enough the *importance of building rapport*, as it allows you to minimise the flakiness of participants and is one of the few variables that you are able to influence. Sometimes, this still won't be enough and you simply have to accept the situation for what it is.

Oftentimes, there will be health-based or practical reasons for participants to withdraw, and these are completely understandable. Obviously, you will be observing all of the appropriate health and safety protocols for your lab, as well as doing your best to understand the needs of participants. Notwithstanding these exceptions, you must appreciate the value of your participant interactions from a human perspective, so that you can maximise recruitment and retention.

Infrastructure

If you are working on a preconceived project, it is highly probable that during its development the logistical implications for you, the student, were the last thing to be considered, if they were even considered at all. The realities of conducting research in a laboratory setting demand space, staff, time, and often specialised equipment. You'll notice that this list fails to mention the participants themselves! Getting all of these ingredients to converge and run effectively for one of many trials is a daunting task at the best of times. It can feel like you're trying to align the planets, to the effect that when everything does click there is a huge sense of relief and reward. It rarely, if ever, goes perfectly though!

From my own experience, several challenges come to mind with respect to infrastructure. One of my studies required trained phlebotomists to obtain blood samples at predefined times, as well as surgeons qualified to obtain tissue biopsy samples. Given the fact that my university did not have an individual trained in-house, but rather a pool of 3-4 staff working on a *pro bono* basis, my testing had to revolve around their availability first and foremost. The staff themselves were excellent, which was a shame given the logistical problems, but efforts to get individuals trained in-house were not forthcoming. Therefore, I averaged three participant completions every six months, meaning that my analysis had to be crammed into several short weeks in tandem with thesis writing. I had no choice but to use the time I should have been testing to work on writing papers and chapters. This was not fundamentally a bad thing, as the bulk of my thesis was written prior to analysis. However, as a PhD student you live and die by the data collection process, it is absolutely integral.

A separate example that comes to mind is the laboratory freezer situation that can be quite common based on anecdotal conversations with students from other institutions. Our freezers were full to the brim with biological samples from a wide array of PhD and staff projects, some many years old and yet to be analysed. Despite this, there was a general reluctance to dispose of these ancient samples, which placed a premium on space. In turn, newly recruited students therefore had limited room to put their precious samples, making it a real challenge not only to store them, but also *find them* to conduct their analyses. If the student took too long sorting them out, the freezer alarm would go off as the temperature rose, so they would have to stop and do something else before returning later on to finish the job. This created a great deal of unnecessary anxiety and stress, as one could potentially damage other students' samples. Eventually, an extra backup freezer was acquired but there was still a two-year period when these issues had to be negotiated.

A third and final example is that of a PhD colleague who was attracted to the institution for a specific research topic. A significant element in her accepting the role was the purported links between the institution and a population group of interest. When she commenced her studies however, there were no such links in place and she had to procure and manifest them of her own accord. This took considerable time and effort to set up, which might be viewed as a useful experience, but ultimately it consumed a lot of valuable resources, the chief of which was time.

My point with these examples is to illustrate that *the infrastructure is not designed for your benefit*, to be brutally honest. Rather, it is designed to benefit the creators, or owners, of the infrastructure. This evokes the sentiments expressed in Chapter 3, highlighting the divergent interests of the institution, its staff, and the student. More PhD students and more staff projects lead to more research, more papers and so forth. This is irrespective of how difficult or stressful it makes life for the present cohort. As a PhD student, you have little power to influence these challenges other than raise them at your supervisory and annual progression meetings, to document them for the record.

A colleague of mine experienced substantial issues with her serum and tissue samples, to the extent that she overran her PhD deadline. This mandated that she seek part-time employment and rely on her husband's income to support her for 12 months afterwards. Indeed, it is fortunate that she had these lifelines, but equally saddening given the challenges she faced. While there were other factors that played a part, it was predominantly the inadequate infrastructure that cost her, as well as recruitment difficulties.

In your role as a PhD scholar, you will be alone for the most part in collecting your data, although this will vary between institutions. This means that you will need to recruit, set up equipment, order consumables, and perform most procedures all by yourself. Although these are invaluable skills (and more on that later), it is imperative that you form strong relationships with your lab and learning support staff. This will make things easier when you need to make equipment requests, order consumables and the like.

The role of other PhD students will be imperative should you need their support, and there is tremendous value in developing a 'collegiate' environment or study group. Learn to compromise with other students through frank and honest discussion, particularly when booking out lab space and equipment. Resolving conflicts through mutual understanding should always be the desired outcome. Fundamentally, it is up to you to make the best of the existing situation and infrastructure to deliver within your remit. You need to position yourself to make the best of the circumstances you find yourself in and keep moving forward, despite the inevitable struggles.

Progression Meetings

As with the COR (Chapter 3), monthly and annual progression meetings are part of the academic 'housekeeping' that needs to be conducted with a substantial degree of regularity. After a while, the monthly meetings may be more sporadic but it is generally best to meet up with your team every couple of months at least. When you are busy with data collection, there is less value in these meetings because you are motoring along with things. In the beginning though, you might meet up every 2-3 weeks for example. These meetings should be documented and a set of objectives formalised for the research office. You won't always meet these objectives, but a 'journey' of sorts should be plotted through the PhD to maintain accountability and focus. If you have a paper trail and keep accurate and up to date records, you will be well positioned should circumstances turn against you. You only get out from your meetings what you put in, so be sure to make use of them. Plan what you intend to discuss and arrive with an agenda!

Annual progression meetings are a bigger deal, involving third-party academic review. Typically, you will attend a meeting with your DoS at the bare minimum, as well as someone from the research office and an academic from a separate discipline within the school. It will be best to provide a short synopsis on the status of your PhD, the major issues of contention, and the primary goals for the following year. These meetings are your opportunity to raise and document concerns whilst acknowledging your successes. Although it would not be appropriate to 'slate' your supervisory team, if you are having considerable issues then this would be a good time to voice them. Following the meeting, your DoS will remain and a discussion will take place to determine whether you can continue to the following year of study. Short of a cataclysmic series of events, it is most likely that you will pass to the next phase and be allowed to move forward with your studies.

6. Data Analysis and Interpretation

Once the data collection phase is complete, you will need to perform reduction and analysis on the raw data to interpret your findings. This phase can take a substantial amount of time, particularly if you have rigorous analytical procedures to perform in the laboratory. There are some broad pieces of advice that I think will be applicable to most students. For instance, it can be very beneficial to type up your data after each trial, as opposed to doing it all at the end. It's much easier to manage things in this way and the student can see their dataset building as they go, which is great for your confidence. You will save a substantial amount of time in this manner, and any downstream analysis of samples can be integrated with the spreadsheet at the end.

The use of biochemical techniques, such as flow cytometry, ELISA, microscopy and so forth should all be optimised before conducting your analysis. The student should be certain that the measures are valid, reliable and evidenced accordingly. A lot of this background work will be performed as part of the planning and ethical review stages, but in terms of testing and validating your assay techniques, this should be performed well in advance of your final analyses. Obviously, the work should be documented in a laboratory handbook and written up in your thesis as part of the methodological development section. There may be variations on this depending on your country of study, institution and/or supervisory team, but there will be commonalities across the board.

As mentioned earlier, it will be optimal to familiarise yourself with the statistical software and data presentation packages you will be using. Whether you use tutorial data or videos is immaterial, *you simply need to have a fundamental understanding* by the time you are in possession of your raw data, to maximise time. The interpretation and statistical analyses themselves will depend on the nature of your PhD and the specific discipline area in which it resides. I won't go into the details of this here, as there are numerous textbooks (see further reading) and resources on the topic. Each student will have their own unique experience and research questions, so the statistical models and interpretation will need to be considered in line with these considerations.

Once you have the core findings mapped out, it can be very useful to schedule a presentation with your supervisory team or colleagues to talk through the data, based on the figures or tables that have been generated. This helps not only with your interpretation of the findings; you may also get valuable feedback and interjections that will inform the writing of papers, in addition to your thesis. What's more, you will develop and enhance your public speaking and critical reasoning skills that will stand you in good stead for the eventual viva voce examination.

7. Writing for Publication and Thesis Submission

As the data collection process concludes and you begin to analyse and interpret your findings, the goal of writing for publication in an academic journal or conference abstract becomes a key focal point. This important step will allow you to establish a reputation in your field and build a portfolio of publications - an essential asset for post-PhD job interviews and an academic career.

The Working Environment

For the reading and writing components of your PhD, as with most levels of academic study, the environment is a crucial variable to consider. I have alluded to some of these aspects in previous chapters, but nevertheless I think it's useful to reiterate some of them here.

During my studies, I found that working in a shared office environment helped me considerably, as I preferred to have some ambient noise, chatter, or music on in the background. You may prefer to work in total silence, and for that the library would be an ideal location. Failing that, you might consider using earplugs to diminish any unwanted noise during periods of intensive work. I know of several former colleagues that used this strategy when they worked in shared offices, and it can be quite effective. A primary advantage of working in a shared office is the sense of camaraderie and the ability to bounce ideas and drafts off colleagues. This can be tremendously beneficial and it helped me massively in the last couple of years of my studies.

I made ample use of pubs and coffee houses, again because of the background noise and vital WiFi availability. The only limitation would be the lack of printing facilities should one need to obtain hard copy publications and the like. In my experience these locations can make a nice change from the office environment and still enable a large amount of work to be done. Much of this depends on your own personality and disposition however. I've known students that never worked at home, and some that never worked at university. Ultimately, you need to find the environment and circumstances that maximise your productivity, preferably earlier as opposed to later.

Academic Journals: The Unit of Currency

Peer-reviewed academic journals will be familiar to all undergraduates and postgraduates, especially those in the biological sciences. In fact, I would query whether a student can complete their undergraduate degree without being familiar with these publications. To establish your reputation and demonstrate scholarship, it will be absolutely essential to get your work published[6]. Like it or not, this process illustrates your ability to write scientifically and pass academic peer review. If your work is well cited and/or shared extensively on social media this will demonstrate the 'impact' that is coveted by most universities these days.

The number of available journals is vast and a considered decision must be made as to which one you

---

[6] https://www.theguardian.com/higher-education-network/2018/aug/09/a-phd-should-be-about-improving-society-not-chasing-academic-kudos.

and your team target, as this will limit stress and confusion later on. The choice will be informed by the aims and scope of the journal, the nature of your article (i.e. review or original investigation) and many other distinct aspects. Once your work has been peer-reviewed and published in a reputable journal, you will have essentially demonstrated the 'worth' of your research findings, as well as their academic credibility and novelty. This can be a huge asset for your viva voce examination and will be something to strive for.

Once you have analysed your data from a statistical standpoint and have generated figures and text from the raw data, an initial draft manuscript should be prepared. Your reference manager (i.e. EndNote) will make this process much easier, as it constructs a bibliography whilst you write. What's more, the specific output style or formatting framework for most journals can be downloaded into EndNote very easily, if it's available. Should your manuscript be rejected at any (highly probable!) point, it's extremely easy to reformat by downloading the alternative journal style prior to resubmission. This saves a tremendous amount of time and effort, and therefore I strongly recommend it.

For scientific research papers, the general format will be familiar to all PhD students from their formative courses. The introduction and discussion sections bookend the article or chapter, with the methods and results serving as the core of the document. You will have a solid grounding in the evidence base from your reading thus far, making the writing of the introduction considerably easier. I found it useful to write the methods first, often when data collection was under way so that the procedures were familiar and easy to describe. This should be followed by the results section, so you have 'what was done' and 'what was found'. The interpretation and rationalisation of the findings in the discussion will be one of the harder sections to write, at least from my experience. Stepping back and thinking objectively about where the findings corroborate with the evidence base can be a real challenge. It's advised that you make use of your colleagues and supervisory team to write this section. Strive to extract the fundamental messages and how they correspond with your research questions.

Ultimately, you will submit the manuscript for peer review to a suitable journal and wait for the editor to send it out to reviewers. Provided there is interest on the part of the editor, the paper will then be sent out for review to a number of peer reviewers, and returned within a variable amount of time with comments and key matters to address. Sometimes these are minor and superficial, whereas others may necessitate wholesale changes to the manuscript. Dealing with the feedback will be a studious and considered process, involving all team members and contributors. Once all of the comments are addressed and the editor and reviewers are satisfied, the paper will be sent for processing and online publication in the first instance.

It's a great feeling seeing your name in print, and once it's out there it can never be taken away from you. When you have a paper accepted you should give yourself a deserved pat on the back and celebrate, as it's a considerable milestone at this relatively early stage of your academic career. These publications will be invaluable as you seek post-PhD employment in either a research or teaching setting. You can track your academic profile using your institutional repository, ResearchGate and other platforms (see useful links). I strongly advise you do this as you can then stay abreast of the impact of your work, based on viewership and citations. It's relatively easy to set up and will be substantially more time-consuming later on if you build up a large body of work.

Conference Proceedings

In contrast with journal articles, conference abstracts are substantially easier to compile. Oftentimes, these are submitted whilst the accompanying paper is being written, to make use of the sometimes lengthy delay between peer review and ultimate publication. At PhD level, the most common submissions to conferences are for oral presentations or poster contributions. The choice between the two will depend on the perspectives of both you and your team, as will the choice of conference to present at. The abstracts are often published in an accompanying booklet and you will be able to add the skills, experience and citations to your portfolio and CV.

Perhaps the most significant value in writing for conference proceedings is the conference attendance itself. Provided you make the most of the opportunity, substantial contacts can be acquired at conferences, in addition to the new knowledge you will gain from the cutting edge of the discipline. Depending on the conference, some can last several days and tend to take place in interesting settings around the world. If you get the opportunity to attend a conference, I strongly advise that you do so as it provides the opportunity to travel and explore, whilst networking with experts in your subject area. Your university will have allocated funding to you precisely for this purpose, and if you fail to spend it then it's usually lost forever. Make the most of the opportunity to explore intriguing cities around the world, whilst promoting your research and building a solid reputation.

The Role of Feedback

With any and all writing you produce during the PhD, the way in which you integrate and use feedback will be a crucial facet. Depending on how many supervisory staff you have on your team, and the number of staff to contribute towards papers and the like, it can be extremely difficult to satisfy all parties. There will be the fundamental elements that are easily adjusted, such as language and prose; however there may be disagreements with relation to data presentation and interpretation. Moreover, the feedback you obtain from one contributor may outright contradict that of another. Therefore, an initial draft that you email through for feedback may splinter off into several other versions, which can be difficult to manage.

These conflicts are magnified when dealing with comments from journal reviewers. For example, there is often a positive linear relationship between the number of co-authors on your paper and the amount of time it takes to collect feedback and approval to resubmit. Do your best to manage these issues and if necessary set reasonable deadlines in your role as the lead author. Sometimes it will be necessary to put your foot down! With thesis chapters there is less pressure as you have more time to sort any discrepancies and iron out conflicts. Also, there are less contributors to worry about as your supervisory team will be the only individuals engaged in this process.

Capitalise on Your Work!

At this moment it will be clear to you that during your PhD studies you will work extremely hard to create what is basically a hard-bound book in a narrow discipline and with a highly specific topic. If there are any opportunities to expose your work in a simpler manner to the wider public, these will be incredibly helpful. I'm not talking about academic exploitation of your graft, such as papers and conferences. Rather, I am alluding to the engagement of the lay public. For instance, I was asked to write a blog post for a former dissertation supervisor that eventually led to an approach by a popular magazine to do a short column for them. With a small amount of *pro bono* work, I was able to get exposure in the printed press and add this experience to my skill set and portfolio.

In your own degrees, you might be able to accomplish the following:

- Conduct an interview with the university press team to promote a research study, as described earlier. This will help not only with recruitment, but will increase the visibility of both you and your institution.

- Compile a press release for local newspapers, radio and potentially television, along similar channels as the previous point.

- Summarise your published articles and findings in an article for your own blog, or a blog in a relevant and specific area of interest.

- Present the findings at workshops and/or gatherings of interested parties and stakeholders. Doing so will enhance your public speaking skills and represents a great networking opportunity.

- Write articles for the lay press and magazines.

The above are just a few suggestions, but they nevertheless illustrate ways of exploiting your hard work and improving your visibility in both the local and wider community.

8. Preparing for the Viva

Your institution will have its own specifications regarding thesis submission and these will be available from the research office and/or the university web pages. Once you have submitted your thesis, you can breathe a sigh of relief given that one of the major hurdles is dealt with. The finale before you are awarded your PhD will be the viva voce (Latin for 'live voice) examination. In the United Kingdom, the viva is an oral examination by at least two reviewers behind closed doors. One will be an internal examiner from your institution, and the other will be an external academic. There will be some choice on the part of you and your team, but nonetheless all examiners will have extensive expertise in your topic area.

A practice viva with members of your team or trusted colleagues will be truly essential, so that you can prepare accordingly. For my own sake I went through mine on two separate occasions and made notes on the probable questions I could be asked. Your project will have abundant strengths and weaknesses that will need to be discussed, so you need to be cognisant of these and annotate them in your thesis. It is best to treat the viva as a developmental assessment, in a similar sense to the COR way back in the beginning. It's not unknown for there to be some hostility or antagonism on the part of the assessors; however the majority will be trying to add value and get the most out of you in the session.

A practice viva is truly essential to run through the process with familiar people and flesh out the major issues. Ask them to be as critical and honest as possible, as doing so will provide the best preparation for the real thing. You might also present your research findings to the academic community at your institution, as this can yield great observations that you may have missed. If you could video the practice viva, that would be extremely useful and is a strategy that several of my colleagues applied. By watching the footage back, you will be able to critique your knowledge, body language and responses to questions from a calm and rational position. This will further enhance your preparation for the real deal!

On the day, ensure that you are alert and focused. Reassure yourself that you have earned the right to be there with years of graft and determination. Your team should provide useful input in the days leading up to the viva. There are some great resources available at Vitae[7] that might help you in your preparation as well. Following the assessment, your examiners will advise the university to award you a PhD with minor corrections (the most common outcome) or may suggest more substantial changes and a timeframe with which to complete them. It is rare that a thesis is accepted with no changes whatsoever, but it certainly can be done!

---

[7] http://www.vitae.ac.uk/.

9. Strategies for Optimal Health and Wellbeing

Annual Leave: Make Use of Your Entitlement

As with any other public or private sector position, you will receive an annual allocation of academic leave and it's vital that you use it. There are no prizes for forging ahead, and if you don't take leave, the days are ultimately lost. In my first 'proper job' as a blue-collar worker it was possible to forego one's holiday allocation and receive the money instead (this would be ideal for a PhD student!) but unfortunately this is not the case in academia. I'm not saying that you need to use all of it, but on an annual basis a significant amount of leave is essential for your physical and psychological health. PhD students are extremely susceptible[8] to mental

---

[8] https://www.theguardian.com/higher-education-network/2018/aug/09/a-phd-should-be-about-improving-society-not-chasing-academic-kudos.

health issues such as depression, so do all you can to mitigate this risk.

It's very easy, once the train has left the station, to forget that you actually have leave 'in the bank'. Psychologically, you become so preoccupied with every facet of the PhD experience. This is primarily because you are cognisant of the limited timeframe. The *train keeps moving* as it were, and it's enticing to preserve precious momentum. Unfortunately, this momentum can also lead to burnout if you don't take the time to rest and recuperate. Ensure that you have at least one good holiday each academic year, preferably to a place that will expand your mind. There are many attractively priced deals to be found, and when you are away *forget about work as much as possible!* In the past I was dismissive of taking leave purely because of the time constraints and financial costs. However, beyond a set point the impact on productivity can be devastating. Take a holiday for the sake of your physical and psychological health!

Develop a Routine

The nature of PhD research is highly stochastic, and this is what makes it so interesting and rewarding.

Therefore, you may benefit from fostering routine in the other aspects of your life. A useful strategy, from my perspective at least, was working in the office, laboratory and coffee shops almost exclusively. I never did any work at home beyond checking my email from time to time. I liked to preserve the home as a location for relaxation and recuperation. If I had to do 14 hour days and work weekends to get the job done, then so be it. I felt a great deal of benefit from working in a shared office, as I like ambient noise when working. Other people may prefer silence, and this is where the library could be an ideal setting. Coffee shops were incredibly valuable to do reading and write my thesis and manuscripts, if only for a change of scenery. If you can get out into nature then you can hit two birds with one stone – do your utmost to explore your surroundings and find areas that provide an optimal work environment.

Another element of routine that I found incredibly valuable was to plan my week on a Sunday evening. Using your calendar application or email, plot your activities for the coming week, beginning with the mandatory ones first (i.e. supervisory meetings, teaching commitments and so on) and then filling in your available slots with other matters. These might be data collection opportunities, manuscript writing, reading and critiquing a research paper, planning your thesis, and basically anything else that works toward your PhD completion. It is also *absolutely vital* that you plan social gatherings as well, such as spending time with friends and family. I'm not saying that you need to follow this calendar as if it were gospel; it should serve as a framework for the week ahead so that you have at least a basic structure. Otherwise, you may fall into an abyss of procrastination that can be very hard to escape from.

Adequate rest is of fundamental importance and should definitely form part of your routine. Different people have their own unique demands and sleeping patterns but whatever you do, ensure that you have a positive environment, free from distractions and electronic devices that may disrupt rest. Whether you are an early or late riser, ensure that you get at least 6 – 8 hours each night, as this will help your cognitive functioning and provide a myriad of other benefits. Get into the habit of assessing sleep hygiene as well, because your environment can pose massive implications for the quality of sleep you ultimately obtain.

Health, Exercise and Nutrition

In keeping with the focus on routine and its general importance, your health, exercise and dietary habits will be of prime importance on the PhD journey. Ensuring you obtain an optimal dietary intake is crucial for maintaining health and mental acuity. Whilst not always practical, it is best to consume a variety of meats (if appropriate based on your disposition), fruit, vegetables, and starchy carbohydrate sources. Without going into the specific details, a diet that provides essential protein, carbohydrates, healthy fats, micronutrients and fluid will be key. Of course, there will be excursions toward junk food and takeaways - these are vital for enjoyment and overall quality of life. In the main however, a diet resembling the above with a focus on *real food* should be the goal. Try to cook properly on six days out of seven, and if necessary prepare food in plastic containers for consumption later on. Not only will this save money, it will optimise your time. The process of cooking can be highly liberating, especially if you have music or a podcast on in the background, preferably on a non-PhD-related topic!

In tandem with your sleep and dietary habits, the role of exercise for your physical and psychological health cannot be overstated. Take yourself on walks in nature and enjoy the local area, contingent on the distance from your accommodation of course. Most campuses will have green and tranquil spaces, as well as some form of countryside within reach. Alongside this, engagement in a sporting activity or gym-based exercise is also essential. For instance, taking part in triathlons and other endurance events was a big passion for some of my colleagues, whereas others focused solely on resistance training. There will probably be room to accommodate both, but the ratio will depend on your own preferences. The primal act of *picking up heavy stuff* confers many benefits, not least increased muscle mass and tone, enhanced bone mass and density, and improved mental health and wellbeing. Specific texts have been included at the end of the book and I highly recommend that you consult these.

The PhD process affects psychological health in a number of ways - it's not uncommon for people to experience high levels of stress, anxiety, frustration and so on. I suggest that you make yourself aware of the support services that are available at your institution, should you need them at any stage. This is also where a strong social group is absolutely key, both for you and your colleagues. Regular physical activity will also be indispensable in this regard, as the health benefits and consistent endorphin release will help release tension.

Engaging in a sport, martial art, tai chi and the like can be a fantastic way to expand your social group whilst having a useful pastime away from the university. Massage, sauna and steam rooms can also be of tremendous value to help relax and unwind after these activities, as can walks in places of great natural beauty, such as National Trust properties for example.

One particular phenomenon that affected me was the so-called 'impostor syndrome' that is fairly common from what I hear. Essentially, the individual doubts their prior accomplishments and believes that they will one day be 'exposed' as a fraud, and are undeserving of their success. The best way to combat this is to recognise your achievements to date, but also act with humility and brutal honesty. You are a PhD scholar because you are there *on merit* and it is important to reinforce this fact. Do so with humility, but also a quiet confidence and this should help mitigate such feelings, or at least it did in my experience. A thirst for knowledge and a genuine passion for improving every day will go a long way towards quelling these fears.

A psychological trap that many students fall into, and it's very easy to do, is to constantly compare themselves to others. The individual observes students in different disciplines or research paradigms, blazing through deadlines and publishing papers, all while they're stuck in the lab struggling with recruitment and hitting brick wall after brick wall. There is nothing to be gained from doing this! If you, as a lab-based student for example, compare yourself to a student conducting a qualitative study using questionnaires, all you will do is depress yourself. Students in these fields often obtain their data rather quickly but then have to spend considerable time deciphering it and interpreting its meaning. However, once the lab-based student has obtained all of their samples the process of analysis can be (but isn't always!) fairly rapid. My main point with this explanation is to advise you to focus on the variables *within your power to influence*, and not waste time and energy worrying about the plight of others in 'better' positions. This is a good philosophy for life in general and can help negate a lot of the anxiety brought about by such counterproductive thinking.

If you take care of the process, the outcome will take care of itself!

Read Widely!

In line with the previous two sections, this habit will form a substantial part of your routine. The act of reading material unrelated to your PhD degree, on regular basis, is a hugely powerful one, and a necessity for life in my opinion. I have found that making time to read for between 4 - 6 hours per week, either at weekends or after work, has added tremendous value to my life. The material you read can be anything – fiction, novels, personal development and finance books, autobiographies and so forth – but it must be unrelated to your PhD. This keeps you grounded in 'big picture' thinking and tremendously enhances your vocabulary. Novels in particular keep you in tune with your imaginative and creative side, which can often get lost in a whirlwind of stats and facts. The end result is a more rounded and versatile intellect, that has great practical application in the wider world.

The academic literature is written in a very unique and specific way, especially in the sciences, and an immersion in this is crucial for PhD success. Nevertheless, it's absolutely paramount that you digest other material for your own health and wellbeing. Since starting my PhD, I've read more books than at any previous time in my life, something that I would never have thought possible in the early phase of my studies. If you only consume scientific papers within the narrow framework of your PhD topic, it's very easy to lose the forest for the trees. I strongly urge you to reap the benefits of conducting wider reading in your own time.

Build up a library of great books, and put the knowledge and prose to good use. Trying to learn something new every day, irrespective of what it is, serves as a good mantra for life more generally. The further reading at the end of this book is a great place for you to start!

Managing Relationships

The challenges of PhD study can place a phenomenal amount of stress on relationships, particularly intimate relationships, given the time investment and commitment involved. I have witnessed the combustion of a number of PhD colleagues' relationships, for a multitude of reasons. Chief among them is that the student's partner is unable to understand or comprehend the nature of PhD study, having never done it before. Thus, it is much more likely that a relationship will stay the course if both parties have experience of the process, due to a sense of 'shared empathy'. For instance, a good friend of mine married a fellow academic during his PhD. There was (and still is) a great deal of mutual understanding between them, despite the stresses he was under at the time. In this case, his partner was a great source of strength and therefore an asset as opposed to a liability. This scenario would be ideal should you seek to foster and develop your own romantic relationships. That's not to say that relationships between PhD students and non-academics can't blossom, but rather that a number of difficulties or conflicts may arise due to the potential absence of empathy and understanding. The same applies for familial relationships, especially if your relatives have never been involved in academia. Do your best to illustrate exactly what your job entails, so that they can truly understand what you get up to on a daily basis.

From my own experience, I decided to focus exclusively on my PhD and look after my own life. Whilst this might be considered selfish, ultimately it is the student that bears the brunt of the stress if they don't complete their studies before the deadline. If anything enters my life then it must be providing value, as my time is incredibly limited, rather than instilling stress and discord. During this period, I simply found that attempting to foster meaningful romantic relationships took a great deal more effort, time and resources than was worthwhile at that stage. It was much more desirable to 'reinvest' that time into activities that offered a tangible and predictable return. With that said, I did a great amount of work to strengthen my familial relationships and support network. Scheduling regular days out, if at all possible, with your social group and/or family is essential for health and wellbeing, as mentioned previously. In dark times, and it is likely that there will be some, you will need this network to fall back on.

10. Risk Parity Principles

In the final year of your PhD programme the levels of stress, fatigue and anxiety can reach a crescendo. This will fundamentally depend on where you are with data collection, analysis and writing, however there will also be a subjective element to this. Discussions with your team and a focus on objective measures of progress will be absolutely key here, as will the management of expectations on both sides. To mitigate such negative feelings, I found a number of principles or strategies that you can apply to help make the final months better for your physical and psychological health.

Build an Emergency Fund

The first task will be to build up an emergency fund of cash that can cover your living expenses for at least three months, ideally six. With most bursaries, if you overrun your allotted time the funding stops, irrespective of whether you have employment lined up or a finished PhD thesis in your hands. I've known a number of students that were so engrossed in their research, or lost time to unforeseen circumstances, that they resembled Wile E. Coyote from the Roadrunner cartoons. They ran off the edge of the cliff, hoping that if they didn't look down they wouldn't fall into the abyss. Suddenly, they had no income to support themselves, and their supervisory team were demanding finished draft chapters of their thesis. These aspects all combined to create massive stress and tension.

An emergency fund will buy you some time while you consider your options and finish writing up. Given that you may not have much spare change from your stipend each month, depending on where you live of course, it's crucial that you regularly put a sum of money away into a savings account, no matter how small. It should be an easily accessible account, but do your best to find the highest available rate of interest. In the present environment, interest rates are pitiful to the extent that your money will be eroded by inflation, but at least you will receive *some* return. The purpose of an emergency fund is not to grow the money, but merely preserve it for when you need it. You may also set up a student account and make use of a 0% overdraft facility, should one be available. This can act as an invaluable buffer should the need arise.

If Possible, Publish!

The main unit of academic currency outside of your degree qualifications is research papers; with quality, quantity, and impact the primary metrics. As highlighted earlier, if you can publish some or all of your research studies before your viva voce examination that will make the process substantially easier. You will have demonstrated peer review by the academic community and this will strongly aid the defence of the thesis. This might not always be possible however, given the issues I've raised earlier in this book. As an acceptable alternative, you should strive to at least publish something, such as a narrative review based on your early thesis chapters. If you are able to collaborate with colleagues on data collection this will also be an indispensable opportunity to co-author a paper and demonstrate your prowess in academic writing. A conference abstract or poster can also be a useful way to get your work out into the community. In doing so, you will demonstrate your skills and knowledge as well as the novelty of your research. This will be beneficial for job applications and should enhance your employability considerably.

Be Accountable and Document Everything

You should make detailed notes on monthly progress meetings and submit these to the research office, following input from your supervisory team. This is a formality that often gets overlooked – make sure you have a paper trail of every meeting and discussion, so that you have accountability should anything go wrong or a dispute arise.

The research training programme (RTP) folder that you will compile during your PhD is a great excuse to do just this. Throw every piece of paperwork from development days, courses and workshops into it and document anything of value. In tandem, track everything electronically so that you can do an honest appraisal of your strengths and weaknesses. You will be able to engage with so many opportunities that you will likely forget what you've done, and this isn't ideal when updating CVs and applying for jobs. Be sure that everything is dated and ordered in a concise and logical manner so it can be retrieved quickly if needed.

Learn to Say 'No'!

The importance of conducting collaborative work with other PhD colleagues can't be understated with regards to your academic development and skills base. However, you should try and avoid getting 'bogged down' in other areas and tasks that essentially drain you of time to work on your PhD. I was guilty of this on several occasions, in that I spent time writing shared papers and collecting data that effectively stole my PhD time away from me. You should perform a cost-benefit analysis from the perspective of hours invested versus the yield, i.e. what will you stand to gain overall? If the return is not worthwhile, you must decline the offer.

The example above depicts a problem of my own making. Contrastingly, some of my former colleagues had to invest substantial time in a large collaborative project for an entire month, and there was nothing they could do about it. They were *compelled* to engage in the project and put their PhD studies on hold. Such a scenario is extremely unsatisfactory, and should be raised with the research office using the appropriate channels. In this case, the return provided to the students was not worth the time and resources invested, and in hindsight the project massively compromised their respective PhDs.

It is imperative that you avoid unnecessary distractions and engage only in non-PhD activities that provide a solid and worthwhile return, without overly hampering your ability to deliver within the allotted timeframe.

Extensions and 'Writing Up'

In certain instances, students will have the ability to request an extension to their studies if circumstances have conspired against them. The university will have a formalised process for bringing this about - you may also raise the issue in supervisory and annual progression meetings. For those on a studentship, typically an extension will not result in you receiving funding beyond the deadline. This is extremely annoying, given that many factors are far beyond your influence to control. Nevertheless, you should receive an agreed extension that will give you more time to complete the research project. I knew students that had to 'go part-time' simply because they ran out of room to manoeuvre. They had to teach for several hours each week and pay for their tuition out of pocket, which was around £2500 per year. Provided the bulk of your research and data collection activities are complete however, you will only need to pay writing up fees, which are far reduced in comparison. The importance of an emergency fund, as mentioned above, can't be understated should you overrun your studentship. If you are self-funding, these concerns are less of a problem in the immediate term.

Consider Employment Avenues Early On

As the deadline for your PhD approaches, the inescapable reality of life without a monthly stipend can *scare you to death*. It certainly did in my experience! Much of this anxiety can be mitigated by applying for jobs six months ahead of time. As mentioned before, you don't want to run out of funding with nowhere to turn so do your utmost to insulate yourself from this problem. The other risk parity strategies outlined above will support you in this aim, as will the tips later on.

If your wish is to stay in academia as a researcher or lecturer, then look for opportunities using the necessary channels (see useful links). Many positions will welcome PhD students with six months or so left on their studentship, as well as those that are writing up their thesis. If your goal is to pursue postdoctoral funding to continue your development and skill acquisition, you will need to allocate significant time to explore this. Discussing post-PhD opportunities with your supervisory team and/or line manager could be a useful exercise. Indeed, there are a range of organisations that might be suitable for your goals, but the requirements and availability of funding is constantly in flux. Based on your discipline area, I suggest seeking advice on this sooner as opposed to later, from somebody with experience in obtaining such funds.

For private sector positions, there is a lot more freedom in terms of when you can apply, in contrast with universities that tend to advertise positions outside of teaching periods. Hence, there are significant periods of low activity, where advertisements are at a premium and nothing much is happening. If a graduate position or private sector job is your goal, for example at a biotechnology or pharmaceutical company, consult their websites and make informal approaches stating your interest, and enclose a quality CV. Applying early is always better than leaving it until the last minute due to other more pressing commitments. To further illustrate how your PhD experience can translate into desirable employment, I have included details on skills/knowledge transfer and career progression in Chapter 11.

11. Enhancing Employability

As you were probably told during your undergraduate and postgraduate education, merely having the qualification is no longer enough to guarantee a job at the end. It is likely that you will have done internships or placements, often for no meaningful wage, in order to enhance your skills and experience to get a PhD position in the first place. Now that you are underway in this endeavour, or still yet obtained your PhD, it is crucial that you maintain a favourable attitude towards personal development and self-improvement. It saddens me to say, but that's just the nature of the environment at present, at least in the United Kingdom.

The 'race to the bottom' has truly taken hold and you must do exemplary things to differentiate yourself from the rest of the herd. As I alluded to in the beginning, more and more people are pursuing advanced degrees and getting their PhDs, which is a good thing from one perspective but negative in others. All of your graft and hardship will, one would hope, result in greater rewards and income for you in the long-term as a result of meaningful and challenging employment. You need to stay hungry and determined, because if you rest on your laurels, someone else will come in and snap up the position.

In tandem with your PhD thesis, your employability can be maximised in a number of ways:

- Publishing your research as you go along (i.e. before your viva) can be invaluable as it develops your academic writing and familiarises you with the peer review process. What's more, you will build a portfolio of papers and begin to cultivate a reputation in your area of expertise.

- Attend conferences (if your funding allows) to present your own work or merely network with other academics in your field. This is absolutely crucial – I have known a number of students that have progressed to post-doctoral positions and the like based on their relationships with external parties. The world runs on networking and 'social capital', so do your best to foster and make use of such opportunities.

- Collaborate with other PhD colleagues within the realms of your discipline. Your ability to do this will depend greatly upon your institution and its culture. I have found that helping other PhD students out is the optimal scenario for everyone, provided there is reciprocity and understanding. Although your supervisory team may attempt to rein you in, *your principle objective is to make yourself as employable as possible* when you finish your studies. The skills and knowledge you will obtain from working with other like-minded students will be indispensable, and you will be able to collaborate on papers so that everybody benefits. Transparency and honesty in this are absolutely paramount, so ensure that you have a mutual understanding with your colleagues.

- Make use of training and development opportunities within your institution. This may take the form of teaching qualifications, seminars and workshops for example. If you are able to learn about new equipment or skills, make use of such opportunities and add them to your curriculum vitae, RTP and/or skills portfolio.

In addition to the above considerations, you need to understand that the PhD itself represents a wealth of *transferable skills and expertise*. In my private sector employment, I knew project managers that didn't do half as much logistical and infrastructure management and planning as I did during my PhD.

Mapping out some of the transferable skills from a typical biological sciences PhD, for example, reveals a tremendous amount of application:

- Compliance with ethical procedures and the production of appropriate paperwork at the university and/or NHS level.

- Justification and defence of research design and procedures in front of a committee.

- An understanding of risk assessment and safety considerations.

- Recruitment of participants through email, leaflets and oral presentations.

- Awareness of stakeholder needs and those of the wider public.

- Critical analysis, evaluation and interpretation of extensive literature.

- Translation of research findings into meaningful statements for the public; so called 'science communication'.

- Experience of teaching at undergraduate or postgraduate level, and therefore proficient in public speaking and communication.

- Knowledge of a wide range of data analysis and presentation software.

- Logistical and infrastructure management, demonstrating strong organisational planning and conscientiousness.

- Competence in numerous laboratory procedures and techniques, using specific equipment and assays.

- Publications in both the academic and lay press.

It is easy to see how these elements have applications across many academic and professional positions, and I urge you to draw up a similar 'skills map' and appraise them for yourself.

12. Closing Remarks

I hope the advice contained in these pages has been both helpful and worthwhile. These tips have been accumulated over a number of years, from my own experience during my PhD and extensive discussions with colleagues. Whilst your own situation may differ based on your institution and circumstances, there will be a great deal of similarity in many areas.

By making use of this knowledge, hopefully your PhD will be a predominantly rewarding and developmental one. As stated in the beginning, completing a PhD will be one of the most demanding and stressful endeavours you are likely to pursue, with a high risk of drop out. It could also be one of the most satisfying and developmental phases of your career. You will experience a tremendous amount of personal and academic growth, in a relatively short period of time. Indeed, my years of PhD study were some of the happiest and rewarding of my life, despite tremendous difficulty at times.

Meeting this challenge is a phenomenal achievement, deserving of high praise, and I wish you every success! Good luck!

Further Reading

Health and Wellbeing

Mindfulness: A Practical Guide to Finding Peace in a Frantic World by Mark Williams and Dr Danny Penman

Starting Strength: Basic Barbell Training (Third Edition) by Mark Rippetoe

Personal Development and Self-Mastery

12 Rules for Life: An Antidote to Chaos by Jordan B. Peterson

Mastery by Robert Greene

Money: Master the Game by Tony Robbins

Principles: Life and Work by Ray Dalio

Statistical and Analytical Methods

Intuitive Biostatistics: A Nonmathematical Guide to Statistical Thinking by Harvey Motulsky

Discovering Statistics Using IBM SPSS Statistics (Fifth Edition) by Andy Field

R for Data Science by Garrett Grolemund and Hadley Wickham

Workplace Dynamics and Relationships

The Art of War by Sun Tzu

The 48 Laws of Power by Robert Greene

How to Win Friends and Influence People by Dale Carnegie

Useful Links

www.academia.edu | *Alongside ResearchGate, serves as a network for scholars*

www.findaphd.com | *A search engine for PhD opportunities*

www.jobs.ac.uk | *Useful for findings jobs in academia as well as studentships*

www.prospects.ac.uk | *Careers guidance and advice*

www.researchgate.com | *Social network for scholars that can yield useful papers*

www.vitae.ac.uk | *Works toward the professional development of researchers*

About the Publisher

Founded in 2018, Rising Tide Press is a small independent publisher of selected fiction, self-help, finance and education titles.

Printed in Great Britain
by Amazon